My Goddess

You are my Goddess
you are my muse
you are the reason I wake up
you are the reason I keep trying even when I want to
give up
I only do what I must when I think of you
I do not do anything illegal since it means I wont see
you
I hold my temper because it would upset you
I do no harm to others because its what you ask of me
But if you even ask me to do the impossible I would
that is how much I love you
I would die for you if that would make you smile
I would kill everyone if that would make you happy
My entire existence is only for you

The Lonesome One

One by one they all leave
one by one they all find fault with him
one by one the lights go out soon his world becomes
pitch black and cold
he sees no one he hears no one he feels nothing
he now knows no one will save him from himself
he starts to wonder where it all went wrong
he wonders who has cursed him
he wonders what he did to deserve this then he
remembers:
He is a demon
he is a monster
he is unwanted
he isn't needed
no one seeks him nor speaks his name
everyone knows that speaking his name will bring upon
terror like none before
he lives alone
he lives in the dark the question remains.
who is brave enough to summon him and save him from
his endless torture and loneliness?

What is Love

Falling in love is the feeling of flying, being on cloud
nine, but at the same time being ground and
relaxed. If you don't feel like that after some time then
that person isn't the one that you were meant to be with
and you should keep searching for your one and only
love. Only then can you be truly and utterly happy

Why I Drank

Today I heard your voice, so I drank
Then I saw your face so I drank again
then I could feel your touch so again I drank
I drank to forget your name
I drank to forget your face
I drank to forget the memories so why is it that no
matter how much I drink I see you
why is it so hard to forget the fun times
why can I not forget the last words I said to you
because I cant forget you I drank
because you meant the world to me I drank
and now because I drank so much we can finally talk to
one another again
because I was wasted I can see your smiling face again
because I was intoxicated by alcohol and love I went on
a drive
because I wanted you again so badly I am with you as
the angels weep over our misfortune
because our love was so strong God couldn't keep us
apart for long

Braveness

Sometime being brave doesn't mean not being scared it
means standing up even when you are scared.
It means to be who you really are when everyone stands
against you.
Its what it means to be human, its apart of humanity.
Being scared is okay but hiding because you are scared
is not okay.
Nothing will change if all you do is hide in a corner.
Be Brave, be yourself and stand for what you believe in
cause even if it feels like the world is against you there
are others out there just like you
so call to them and stand tall and brave together as one

My Love for you

These feelings keep growing and make me more
unstable, more aggressive, more impatient and more
unwilling to deal with this life any longer without you.
My world becomes nothing more than a deep Black
hole with no escape when I didn't know you. Just
when I was going to give up and give in to the darkness
you came. You became a light that's stronger than any
sun or moon in any universe. You are like billions and
billions of Stars that   lead me in the right direction and
you are the only one who keeps me safe and sane as the
world tries to rip me apart and that is why I love you so.

I Thank You

As I sit alone in my dark room my thoughts overflow
They go haywire and storm about
As if my thoughts have turned into a Texas tornado and
taking things apart
As I try to make sense of them, you come to mind
You are the one who helps me keep my sanity
You help to keep my thoughts in control
You have become my sole reason to understanding this
world
You are my love, and my life
I thank you from the bottom of my very soul for being
by me
I thank you for helping me defeat my demons
I thank you for all that you do
I thank you for loving even a monster as horrible as me

<u>*Be the True You*</u>

People always tell you to be prepared
They tell you to make sure of yourself
they tell you to not ask questions
they tell you to listen
they tell you to behave
They tell you that you have to act a certain way
they will tell you to be respectful
they will tell you to mind yourself but have they ever
told you to dream
have they told you its ok if you don't know something?
have they told you its ok to say no?
 that its ok to not understand?
that you don't have to be perfect?
that you can have your own beliefs?
that you can be who you are and you wont be judged?
Has anyone ever said that to anyone?
I've always been told to be myself and do my best
I have always been loved no matter what I did or how
badly I messed up
In a world full of pure hatred and non acceptance, I as
the freak I am
Have always been loved
Have always been kind
have always been caring and was taught to accept
others as they are and for who they are
So why cant the rest of the world also do that?
Is it so hard?
is it something that must be taught?
where has the humanity in human gone?

The Sun, The Moon, The Sky

When it rains, I think the sky is sad and crying
 It is sad because it looks down at the earth
It sees how its broken and sick
It sees how broken and sick the humans have become
The sky weeps for the people as they hurt and kill one
another
It weeps as the people curse the sky for not enough rain
It cries harder when it is cursed for giving too much
As the people rant and curse the sky they don't see the
damage they are doing
They don't notice how alone and depressed the sky now
is
And so as the sky cries the sun and moon move closer
They wish to help there dear friend
They wish for the Sky to no longer feel alone
And as they move closer they curse the humans
They move closer and closer
They slowly start killing the humans and the planet
They wish for the sky to go back to them and be happy
like he used to be
 they want him by their side and to no longer look down
and as the sky turns his head toward his old friends, the
humans vanish
The sky is once again happy
The moon and sun regret nothing as they see their
friend smile again for the first time in millennia

<u>Nature</u>

The tall mountains
the beautiful green trees
The large glistening blue lake
Nature is wonderful its beautiful its magnificent
but at the same time its dangerous
Rocks the size of airplanes, falling from a high cliff
Avalanches happening without any actual cause
Nature can kill
As beautiful as she is, she can end your life quicker then
you wish
Being curious and searching for things is fine
But one must be cautious of Natures true form and true
emotions
because if you aren't careful
Nature will bite you in the ass and end you quickly

<u>*For Love*</u>

Because you are the reason I breath the reason why I
don't kill everyone and everything
 you are the reason I have yet to go insane due to my
own darkness
 you are my light in my darkest day and my moon when
I see no stars
I tread upon this earth only for your sake and let it live
for your sake
That is why I am kind to you as should all those on this
god forsaken planet
they are only alive thanks to you so they should all bow
before you and kiss your feet for you are the true
goddess of this world my love
so never forget that

<u>The Hero</u>

In times of chaos and greed Only the true hero of
humanity will rise
As everyone kills each other the Gods watch in
amusement
They find it amazing how incompetent the human race
is
They laugh at the bloodshed
They make jokes at the desperate calls for help
That is when the hero rises
He brings the humans their humanity back
He heals the broken
He helps to bury their dead
He roams the lands as the new light for humanity
Again the Gods are amused
This hero is not from the Gods
he spreads a message throughout the lands
his message angers the gods
the people protect and follow the hero
The people love the hero
He leads them in their time of need and after he is
finished helping them
He leads them to Hell and the demons
For that is where his master waits
That is why the Gods hate
The hero plans to steal their fun
and so now Humanity is gone

<u>The meaning behind True love</u>

As the sun sets and the moon rises
Billions of stars come to greet you tonight
My thoughts greet you as you look to the moon
My soul sings as I realize soon we will be together
again
I thank the heavens for showing us a new path
And as we tread this new path we do so together
We walk hand in hand and look at all the beauty
surrounding us
we talk and laugh
We have fun as we continue the long journey
As we continue I feel you grow weaker
I feel you slowly fading
And as I can no longer feel, see, smell, or sense you I
know
I know that you are no longer amoungst the living
I know that your soul has been called back to our
creator
I continue to travel alone
Slowly my will to go on fades
 I sit alone on this path
I sit alone in the forest we built as we kept on moving
I have no one
No one needs or wants me either
I sit here and wait for my mate
I wait for them to return to me
I will stay here as a lost soul till my lover is reborn
I will forever remain here waiting for that my dear ones
is the true meaning behind true love

What are Dreams?

What if the dreams we see as we sleep are visions of a
reality in which has yet to come
Or visions of a future we didn't know was possible
Maybe that is why some cant remember their dreams
It is the heavens way of telling us, they do not want us
to even try for those dreams
I say, Why not?
Be brave, be bold, be you and remember
The future you wish for will not come if all one does is
listen
The future we wish for can not be obtained from
wishing others would do it for us
We cant count on others to show us our way
we must pave the road to greatness with our own hands
We are strong enough, so why wait?
we were made to think for ourselves so why ask
permission to change our own lives?
Why ask if its ok to be our true selves?
 Why let others dictate our lives when they don't even
know us?
Fate and Future belong to you, yourself so make the
best of everyday
fight for the future you wish for, even if the world is
against you
For you never know when it will be your last

True Friends are like a Wolf pack

The world is only as dark as the people you keep by you
If you feel like your world is becoming black take a
look at who is by you
Look to those you call friends
The ones who truly like you, will help you
The ones who don't, will try to make your problems
seem smaller then theirs
The real friends, will come to you and help you out of
your darkness
no matter the time or place
The ones who ignore you are not even worth your
valuable time
You need to take care of you
and if all you have is toxic friends then my advice to
you is to leave them
Because when you are truly alone that's when you
notice the true brightness of the world   That is also
when your true friends will come crawling out of the
cracks to be by your side why waste your precious time
on good for nothing idiots who only bring you down?
It is in human nature to look for those who can be in
your pack
But sometimes even a wolf will need his alone time to
find who his true friends really are don't give up the
fight, for this lone wolf is also on your side, even if you
don't know it

You wont be needed

I find myself thinking of our lost time
I think of all the fun times we couldn't have
I think of all the times I couldn't be there
I think of all the times I needed you
I think of all the times I could have cried on your
shoulder
I think of all the times I wanted your love
now all I think about is how you never wanted me
I think of the time I heard you say I was useless
the time you said I am not wanted
the time you said I am not needed
the time you called me a fat pig
the time you called me an idiot
the time you had raised your hand but let it slide
the time I cried and you said they were fake tears
the time that you said I shouldn't have been born
and now you come to me wanting me
you want my money
you want my fame
you want to be my parent
you want to be part of my life
but I don't want you
I don't want your fake love
your fake words
your fake smile
you and your lover can stay away
I am strong
I am independent
I am loved
I am needed
I will never in this life or the next need you

Darkness isn't Good

in the darkness we find our friends
some find that their demons are better friends than
humans
some find that their demons are kinder
their demons make more sense
and slowly they slip deeper into their darkness
the darkness calls to them
its starts to feel warm and safe
it makes you feel like the real world isn't worth it
it tells you to stay
it tells you you are safe
the demons slowly eat away at your soul
and when you try to break free, you find yourself
suddenly falling
you fall and fall
no one can save you
no one can help you
but who is to blame?
is it the parents that didn't notice?
is it the friends who never asked?
is it the Gods who wished to bring back an angel?
No, its none of them
the person to blame is the one who didn't notice that the
darkness isn't a friend
its the person who tried to run away too late
its the one who is now falling to their death
don't always trust your demons
don't trust in humans too much
because no matter what in the end the only person to
blame for everything is you

so don't let the demons tell you how you need to live
decide for yourself
be yourself
power on and live in the light
because even when the darkness feels warm
its not a safe kind of warm
its the warm you feel before your body lets go of
everything and you become cold

Love at first Sight

Why do they call it falling in love at first sight?
its because even though you just met you feel a strong
connection
you looked at each other and felt the world stand still
you saw one another and the world went quiet
you felt like the part of you that was missing finally
showed up
You notice after a while that they are what make you
perfect
you notice that everything about them drives you crazy
you find yourself falling deeper into love
you are happy with just being near them
you are beyond yourself with how they make you feel
and suddenly the world goes dark
you feel the sky fall
you see everyone wearing black
and as you cry, you feel yourself break
you don't feel like going on
you wish the world will end
but its not the end of the world
you have to get back up
you have to go back out into the world
because if you don't you will miss your chance
you wont find that happiness again by staying indoors
you wont find it in your books
you wont find it in your art
it wont be in your movies
its outside
its where other beings are
so get up and try to fall again
because that's the only way to being happy once again

Careful with your words

A million thought run through my head
I hear what you say
I know what you mean
A part of me wants to run away
Another part wants to show you
I want to show what I can do
I want to let you hear my thunder
I want you to hear my mighty roar
But the other part of me.....
It says your right
It tells me to stay hidden
It tells me to not try
It tells me to play it safe
After one is told they aren't good enough
It stays in the mind
It keeps them from trying
It keeps them from wanting
It drags them down
So as the million thoughts keep me awake at night
Before you speak, think twice
It could save a life

Busy Hospital

As I sit and wait I see many people running by
Some sweating
Some crying
Some looking defeated
Some wondering where God is
Some sitting like me and waiting
As we wait we pray
We pray for health
We pray for good news
We pray for gods mercy
As we finish our prayers a nurse walks in
She looks tired
She looks like she went through hell
She calls my name and as I stand I can see she had cried
I pat the nurse on the shoulder
I tell her its fine
I tell her you cant save them all
I smile at her, give her my blessings and go home
I sit in my chair
I look at your picture
Sometimes God needs his angels back
Sometimes your in the wrong place at the wrong time
Sometimes as a nurse you get blamed for a death
Sometimes that persons family wants revenge
Sometimes even your colleagues cant save you
So be kind to everyone
You don't know what demons they fight
And you don't know what wars they are battling

What Happened to Humanity?

I sit and listen to conversations in my favorite Pub
I listen to stories
I listen to opinions
I listen to Arguments
I listen to laughter
I listen to heartbreaks
I listen to the music
as I listen I hear a small cry
I look over my shoulder
I see a young girl
I see her crying face
I see how hurt she is
I feel how hurt she is
I get up
I walk over
we talk
I calm her down
I comfort her
She cries some more
she is moved by my kindness
She tells me her story
she tells me she is sorry
I smile and tell her:
Its nothing to be ashamed about
everyone has their moment of weakness
as humans we should help those around us
we should help those who need us
no matter for what reason
its saddens me that humans have forgotten what love is
it saddens me that humans forgot how to help others
it saddens me that humans are only greedy and can only
hurt others

I wish humans would go back to caring
I wish they would stop killing others without reason
I wish the wars would stop and girls like you would no
longer have to cry alone
but sadly humans get worse by the day
they only know how to hate
and that's why the planet is dying, but no one truly cares
I sit and listen to conversations in my favorite Pub
I listen to stories
I listen to opinions
I listen to Arguments
I listen to laughter
I listen to heartbreaks
I listen to the music
as I listen I hear a small cry
I look over my shoulder
I see a young girl
I see her crying face
I see how hurt she is
I feel how hurt she is
I get up
I walk over
we talk
I calm her down
I comfort her
She cries some more
she is moved by my kindness
She tells me her story
she tells me she is sorry
I smile and tell her:
Its nothing to be ashamed about
everyone has their moment of weakness
as humans we should help those around us
we should help those who need us

no matter for what reason
its saddens me that humans have forgotten what love is
it saddens me that humans forgot how to help others
it saddens me that humans are only greedy and can only
hurt others
I wish humans would go back to caring
I wish they would stop killing others without reason
I wish the wars would stop and girls like you would no
longer have to cry alone
but sadly humans get worse by the day
they only know how to hate
and that's why the planet is dying, but no one truly cares

<u>*A Lost Love*</u>

Sometimes when I look up at the night sky
I see the stars
I watch them glow
I start to think of home
I start to wish to leave this place
I want to be next to you
I realize how far away you are
I realize how much I have lost
Now all I wish is to be by your side
I no longer wish to stay all alone here
So I go on an adventure
I am now a star too
But even so I am far from you
but now I can see you more clearly
I can hear your voice
I can hear you laughing
I find peace in the black space between us
I am happy just being this much closer to you
and as you turn and smile at me
as you shine so brightly
I am happy that I can at least watch you and see you
from afar

Dark Thoughts

As I lay and stare at the ceiling I realize somethings
I realize I am no longer happy
I realize I am not where I wish to be
I realize I am not who I wanted to be
Slowly my thoughts go deeper
Why?
Who is at fault?
Who needs to change?
What needs to be changed?
again they go deeper and now darker
Its my fault
Its my fault that I am unhappy
Its my fault that nothing changes
Its my fault that my world is falling apart
Its my fault that I am not as loved as I wish to be
Its my fault, everything is all my fault
Then a tiny voice in my head, starts to grow louder
You did this
You are at fault for the family falling apart
You are at fault for speaking
You are at fault for their deaths
You are the monster
You are the one who needs to go away
The voice gets louder and louder till it screams
Die
That's the only way
You need to go away for good
You need to disappear
If only you were never born

If only you wouldn't exist
If only you would have died that day
My heart starts to agree with the thoughts in my head
If you die then you wont feel pain
You wont get sick
you wont have to fear of saying the wrong thing again
So I quietly lay in my bed
I lay there, staring blankly at the ceiling
I am unable to cry
I start to sink into myself
I turn off everything
I no longer wish to be a burden
I no longer wish to work so hard
I no longer feel myself necessary in anyone's lives
I close my eyes
I take a deep breath
I wait for death to come
but again he walks by me and takes someone else
He doesn't want me either
No one wants the cursed being
no one cares for it either
I am forever alone
And forever my mind will tell me that I am not worth
the effort
It will forever tell me to die
And as I wake up and wish for death
He smiles and shakes his head
Not yet child, not yet
You have much to do
Even if you are tired
Even if you are broken
You must carry on

<u>*A Sunny Day*</u>

As I walk through the woods, the sun shines down
I can feel its warmth
A small breeze goes through the trees
I let my mind wander as I bask in the suns warmth
I can feel myself becoming calm
I come to an opening in the forest
I sit down while looking up at the sky
I lay in the soft grass
I watch the planes and birds
I wish this moment would last forever
As I lay I listen to the birds sing
I listen to the laughter of bypassers
I listen to the animals
I wish to lay here forever
And as I take in the warmth and peace
I forget about all of my worldly problems
I forget for a small time about my pain
I forget about my worries
I forget about everything and just rest
For the sun is my only friend
He helps to remind me to take a breather
Because no matter what my problems wont run away
They will only go away after taking everyday one step
at a time.
So sit down, relax, take a breather, and take every
problem one step and one day at a time
otherwise they will only get more complicated

Herstellung und Verlag: BoD – Books on Demand,
Norderstedt
ISBN: 9783755798309